EASY

EVERYDAY

SPANISH

**LINDA
SHEPHERD**

Easy Everyday Spanish: copyright © Linda Shepherd,

January 2008

Registration No.293199084 (IPRO, CRS)

The author asserts the moral right to be identified as the author of this

work.

ISBN:978-0-9559772-1-3

The Author

Linda Shepherd is an Honours Graduate of London University in Spanish and Latin-American Studies with extensive experience in both Britain and in Spain, ranging through primary, secondary and further education field; she was, in addition, a successful primary head teacher in the north of England.Although work most of her language teaching experience had been in the TEFL field, she began a very successful phase in her

career when she decided to work in TESOL.

Career details:

1965-65: TEFL assistant, Mangold Institute, Madrid.

1965 -77:Primary and middle school assistant.

1977-80:Head Teacher.

1983-86: TESOL assistant, Oxford School, Panton St., London, WC1.

1986,87: Head of Oxford School Summer school,

Brighton Polytechnic.

1987-89: Head of Business English, The English

School, Seville.

1989-92: Advisory Primary Teacher, Greater

Manchester.)

CHAPTER ONE

You want to learn Spanish?

Not as difficult as you may think!

First of all just ask yourself these two questions:

1. Can I sing or hum a tune after I've heard it once or twice?

2. Do I really want to learn?

If the answers to both questions is 'YES' then it really will be easy!

There are just one or two things to say before YOU get started.

Someone may have told you that Spanish pronunciation is difficult but it is in fact easier than English pronunciation. Compare these two words:- bear (the animal), - fear (state of being afraid). That difference in pronunciation cannot occur in Spanish.

Spanish Sounds:

There are rules, however - just as in anything -so:

1. 'C or Z' before ' i / e ' sounds like 'th'

(try 'cinco' - five [theen-koh] or 'cerrar'-to close [theh-rar]

2. 'LL' sounds like 'y' ('llave' - key [yah-veh]

3 'J' sounds like 'ch' in Scottish 'loch'. It can be a soft K + W: 'Juan' [kwan]

4. 'Ñ' sounds like 'ni' in 'onion' [señor-mister, sir]

All right so far? Good, now keep repeating to yourself,

'Spanish is NOT difficult' In fact it is EASIER than French, German or even Italian, so as for making yourself understood

FORGET ABOUT GRAMMAR and LONG LISTS

OF VERBS. THAT IS THE GOOD NEWS...The bad news?

YOU WILL NEED TO MEMORISE!!!!

HERE'S HOW:

1. Write the word down.
2. Write it again - slowly this time, and say the letters as you write.
3. Shut your eyes and imagine a white screen in front of you...now see the word in **BIG BOLD CAPITALS. HOLD THAT IMAGE AS LONG AS YOU CAN.**
4. Keep your eyes closed and using one finger trace the word on the table (or surface) in front of you. Now move around your room (or your space) and trace the same word on three different surfaces (you can open your eyes for this) and as you trace, say the letters of the word.

5. Repeat step 4 but move out of your space, out of the room, or the house and do it until you feel you have it 'locked' in your head.

6. If you are trying to memorise an everyday object, say, a cup or an apple, then hold the object in your hand while you say the word (taza, manzana) and at the same time explore the object - its colour, its shape, size and texture.

You may ask, "Why do I have to do this? Surely all I need to do is look, write and repeat the word." While that may be true for some people, we are using a vital learning process here, something I will explain as we go along. But try the six steps to memorising.

They do work. You may feel stupid doing them, but I can assure you they DO work, and more importantly, doing them will make your learning so much easier.

Now, wherever you are, take a look at yourself and write down what you can see.

SHOES................ZAPATOS [thah-pah-taws]

SHIRT............CAMISA [kah-mee-sah]

BLOUSE.........BLUSA [bloo-sah]

TROUSERS.....PANTALONES [pahn-tah-law-nehs]

(Think of 'pants')

In the pronunciation example for the last word, you may have noticed that I used 'law' for the 'lon' part of the word. WHY?

Because all Spanish vowel sounds (a, e, i, o, u) are pure sounds, there are no blends as in English ('au' – taught: 'ou'- fought...and so on).

'A' is always...'ah' .... padre [pah-dreh] - father

'E' is always...'eh' ....leche [leh-cheh]-milk

' I' and 'Y' are always...'ee'........limonada[lee-maw-nah-dah]

8

'O' is always 'aw' ....It is NOT the English 'o' as in 'so-so'.

'por' – for, sounds like [pawr]

'U' is always 'oo' ....'muy' [moo-ee]

From now on I will put 5 simple, everyday words at the beginning of each chapter. Make the effort to memorise them, following the steps 1-6 on pages 2 and 3 and then at the end of each chapter, we will have a test.

Let's start with a mini-test to see how many of the words from this chapter you can recall. You've seen 15 Spanish words and if you've remembered all of them, that's a brilliant start to your first lesson. If you can't remember all of them (but I doubt that! and it is only your first lesson!) you will do better next time. Let's get started.

Put a circle round the words that you know in the following list:

limonada, vino, leche, cerveza, agua.

2. What do all the following words have in common? (Yes, I know they are all Spanish. Think of another connection). And just to exercise your brain...circle the odd one out[do that first!].

Pantalones, camisa, musica, blusa, zapatos

3. Fill in the blanks in the following words:

ll * * e : key   t * z * : cup

   m *n z * n * : apple   c * n * o: five

CHAPTER TWO

Your 5 words.

1. leche (you know its meaning AND how to say it)

2. pan - use your dictionary if you must.

3. vino (Come on. We all know it and love it).

4. queso (keh-saw) Look it up in your dictionary, then do the memorizing drill. THAT'S REALLY IMPORTANT- SO NEVER MISS IT.

5. té (teh) Look it up.........The British national drink!

Now think about two things (1) how you learned to speak English and (2) what English sounds like.........I'll explain that last statement later.

(1) You did not come into this world speaking English, nor carrying an English grammar book and neither did either parent give you grammar

lessons. Your learning tools were (and still are!)   B E E B!

What does BEEB stand for?

B - BRAIN; E - EYES; E - EARS : B - Body (legs, hands, fingers, etc.)

So what I am trying to tell you is, IN LEARNING Spanish – BE ACTIVE,

USE the BEEB.

(2) Every language has its own rhythm as well as its own sounds.

A Spanish friend of mine, a computer programmer from Madrid complained that English is ' cut and dried, it doesn't flow. It's very like German' .

Think of how you speak this sentence, try and listen to yourself saying it.

"What are we having for dinner this evening?"
YOU DO NOT PRONOUNCE EACH WORD INDIVIDUALLY.

The 'flag' or 'cue' word/ word parts are,

"What...we...have...(dinn)...ev...ing"

Why have I not reproduced every part of every word?

Because in normal conversation we use language clues or word 'flags'.

Why am I going into details here and maybe boring some of my readers.

BECAUSE TO LEARN A LANGUAGE, you must know how it works, how to REALLY listen to it, to its rhythm and to its 'clue'words. There are 2 ways to help you along that road:

(1)listen to Spanish (find a Spanish radio station – easy if you live there.)

;get hold of a Spanish conversation tape- Sky do/did have a Spanish TV slot.

If/when you are in Spain, REALLY listen to people

talking. You will be surprised at how many words you recognize – especially after using this book.

Now here are some useful expressions using common verbs:

ESTOY..........I am.....(temporary state- 'estoy en mi casa' means 'I'm at home' (just for now).

SOY...........I am.......(unchanging - soy americano....I always will be...).

QUIERO [kee-eh-raw].....I want, I'd like: quiero pan -I'd like some bread.

ME FALTA [meh fahl-tah]...I need, I am lacking...Me falta vino - [meh- fahl-tah vee-naw]- I haven't got any wine.

Let's just go with those 4 basic expressions, and see if you can make sentences with them + the words in your daily 5 list, OR any of the words you NOW know, e.g.,

Me falta leche, etc., etc.

Have a break from reading this and write down as many sentences as you can and WHILE you write, SPEAK THEM. That really is important. It will speed up your learning. Better still, record yourself if you can get a Dictaphone (mobile phone?) or something similar.

Put your sentences on one side and let's look back. See how much you've learned, but think how many Spanish words you already knew. Think of, ' paella, vamos (from the Westerns we've seen)mantilla, cigar (from "cigarro,' Can you add to that short list?

That brings me to the MOST IMPORTANT part of this book. When I spoke about learning Spanish, I said ANYONE CAN DO or LEARN ANYTHING (within reason) AND SO........YOU CAN (and WILL) LEARN SPANISH.

At this point you may ask, "What prevents me from learning?

There are many reasons but I single out two. Fear and lack of incentive.

FEAR: We make excuses for ourselves, we are afraid to make the necessary effort, afraid of failure. This book is different from a phrase or course book because I try to give you FAITH, the faith in yourself, faith that you can do what you want to do.

LACK OF INCENTIVE: I have always wanted to learn Chinese but why should I? I will never go there, or if I do it will be as part of a guided tour. My days of backpacking are over. But if I live in a foreign country and intend to stay there, then I surely have sufficient motivation to learn its language.

Look back at 'quiero' [key-eh-raw]. Go through the memorizing drill on pages 6 and 7 and then put 'quiero' with the following words to make sentences:-

una casa, una camisa, un libro, pan,

cerveza [thehr-veh-thah] vino [vee-naw].

When you have done that (and are happy with the result) sit back and think about all the words and expressions you have learned so far - shut your eyes and try to recall them –

WE NEVER TRULY FORGET ANYTHING.

They are words you will hear in Spain or they are connected with shopping or ordering in a bar. Write down as many as you can recall.

CHAPTER THREE

Your daily 5 list is:

calle [kal-yeh] street, correos [kaw-reh-aws] post office, sellos [seh-yaws] stamps, vender [vehn-dehr] to sell,

comprar [kawm-prahr] to buy.

They should be easy to learn as there is a connection between all/most of them. Once you have MEMORIZED them, go on and do this quick test:

Write down the Spanish for: bread, shirt, beer, wine, I want, I need.

If you didn't get all 6, no pasa nada (' it's no problem.'). Try again in a few hours' time.

Let's look at counting and here I am asking you to do the work - (you will remember what you learn because YOU are involved).

Look in your dictionary for the numbers below, and then do the memorizing drill.

Let's start with 1 to 10.

1. ***: what about the Fiat model? (NUMERO * * *)

2. ***   3.**e*   4.c * a* * * o

(think of 'quarter'

5. * * * * o: you know this one. Think!!!

6. s e * s [pronounced seh-ees]

7. s i * t * [see-eh-teh]

8. o * * o (Easy? [pronounced 'aw-chaw']

9. n * * v * [pron. noo-eh-veh]

10. d * * z [pron. dee-eh-th]

In this chapter I have given you some new words. Because I KNOW you can learn them. All you have to do is just WANT to do it and BELIEVE that you can. These 2 mind-sets are necessary for you to succeed. To test that, fill in the blanks below:-

5 stamps: c - - - -   s - - - - -

3 streets: t - - -   c - - - - - -

The post office: el c - - - - - -

Now try to make these sentences:

I am in the post office. E - - - -   en   e-   c - - - - - -

I am a teacher. S - -   p - - f - s - r (Yes! It is like the English word.)

I need stamps. M -   f - - t -   s - - - o -

I want 6 stamps. Q - - - - o   s - - s   s - - - o -

I am in the street. E - - - y   - -   la   c - - - -

CHAPTER FOUR

Your list of 5 is:

Voy : I go [it rhymes with 'soy, and 'estoy']

Voy de compras [vaw-ee deh kawm-pras] I'm going shopping.

Doy : I give / am giving

Bebo [beh-baw]: I drink/ am drinking

Como [kaw-maw] - I eat/ am eating. So for example, ' bebo cerveza' means that I usually drink…/ I am drinking beer.

"Bebo cerveza cada día" ('cada' means?? Use your dictionary!)

Mañana [pron. mah-nee-yah-nah]….tomorrow, morning.

Here is a sentence I've made using the

words/phrases on page 21,

"Voy de compras hoy."

Use your dictionary for that last word.

Now you can write what the sentence means.

It's time now to talk about verbs......If I could avoid using the word 'verb', I would, but to tell the truth, the word itself only means 'word' in Latin. We British tend to think that Spanish verbs (or ANY verbs are difficult). I have had so many students of Spanish who have complained,

"I can cope with everything except the verbs. It's

those long lists that throw me!"

Are Spanish verbs all that difficult? My honest answer is YES and NO. The trouble is that languages like French, Italian, German, and Spanish (and many more) have very organized grammar.

But what is grammar? The word comes from a Greek word meaning 'something written' and I suppose grammar really means the rules we follow when writing or speaking.

English grammar does exist and was taught in schools but like so many things it was thrown out of the curriculum (the teaching programme) in most English schools. Why? I suspect because it was difficult to make it interesting, but unlike most continental languages, English has developed a FLEXIBILITY that involves either breaking or bending the rules.

In English you can say, for example, 'horse box' but if you translated that into Spanish it would be 'caballo caja' which would be nonsense to any Spaniard! So to sum up....YOU MUST OBEY THE RULES IF YOU WANT TO SPEAK PASSABLE SPANISH.

There are quite a few rules to learn, but I'll keep them simple and only give you what you need. Let's get a few things straight:

Rule1. In Spanish you often only need 1 word where in English you would need 2 or more. Here are some examples:

SPANISH	ENGLISH
Quiero	I want
Doy	I give/ am giving
Voy	I go /am going
Estoy	I am
Estás	You are
Está	He/She is

Now you will have realized that it can't be all that simple to learn Spanish…BUT it is NOT difficult, once you learn a few EASY rules. We'll pick up on pronunciation along the way (as we have been doing) and any grammar you need will be explained clearly and simply. I ask the question again…what is grammar? Yes, I know…Boring, boring….But that's only because we haven't realized that it's just like texting on your mobile. Let's suppose you want to send a message to your friend to say – "It will be great to see you tomorrow at eight-o-clock." Can you improve on? " Will b gr8 2 c u 2morrow."

Many of you could make it shorter but the important point is that in texting, we use a simplified form of words and spelling, rather like what used to be called ' shorthand' (secretaries used it when taking dictation from their bosses.) So the terms we use in grammar are just a shorthand/simplified way to describe what we are talking about.

If your car or motor bike has broken down it will help you or the mechanic if you use the correct names of parts you are talking about,

e.g., carburettor, big end, oil filter….if you can then say to the mechanic, "I'm having trouble with the carburettor.", he will know where to start. In the same way, grammar is a shorthand way of talking about words…and that is all.

I promised to make things easy for you, and I will have to use 3 words – noun, verb, adjective. The first two are easy to understand so let's start with the first, ' noun'.

That word is a naming word (from Latin "nomen" – think of 'nominate')- it names things and examples of nouns are – boy, box, car.

Verbs!! Think back to school days. " A verb is a doing word"?

I have always added a bit more to say, " A verb is a doing, being or having word." And that covers everything. So ' I run, he has, she is ' are all verbs. If all that is not clear, read the last two pages again until you really understand.

Now for "adjective" and this is really easy, and again I'm sure you remember that from schooldays - a 'describing word' and I can't improve on that. An adjective tells you about nouns, how big, small, what colour, etc. and so 'tiny, huge, green, scary' are all adjectives.

We really don't need any more rules, so let's get started.

Nouns in Spanish are easy to learn – it's pure memory work, and you already know quite a few…cerveza, vino, paella.

Make a list of at least 10. Or better still have a game with your partner, see who can get the biggest number of nouns. Most nouns end in either 'a' or 'o' If they end in 'o' they are nearly always masculine while those ending in 'a' are usually feminine (but not always (idioma, idea).

Put the nouns in the following list into the two columns below:-casa, banco, taza, zapato, blusa, comida, toro, cama, dinero, diario, sabana, vino, torero.

MASCULINE   FEMININE

There are just 2 other things to mention, and you will find them EASY and USEFUL!

1. A, AN, THE :

   Just as in English we say, 'I have a book' or 'she is looking out of the window' so in Spanish we have to use 'un'(a,an) for masculine words and 'una'(a,an) for feminine ones; we also have to use 'el' [the] for masculine words and 'la'[the] for feminine ones.

Try this little test.

Put 'el/la' with these words: …cerveza, …vino, …zapato, …camisa, …banco.

Put 'un/una' with these words:

…diario, …taza, …comida, …toro, …cama.

P.S. If there were ANY words in the above lists that you did not know, USE your dictionary.

CHAPTER FIVE

Your 5 words: rico - (ree-kaw): pobre – (paw-breh):

bueno (boo-weh-naw): hombre – (awhm-breh):

grande – (grahn-deh).

I hear you say, "You haven't given us the meanings!"

Well, no. I want you to guess or use your dictionary. Don't worry you'll get them all right.

ADJECTIVES: You know that these words give you information about things, animals or people – big, good, rich, fat.

So what does "Es un hombre rico" mean?..

Es un perro grande……………………..

Es un día bueno…………………………

Es una mujer rica………………………

Es una taza grande………………………

Es una comida muy buena…………………

DO YOU SEE THE CHANGE?

If a noun is masculine, its adjective is too and the same goes for feminine nouns. Here are some everyday adjectives, but I'll leave some blanks for you to work out.

MALO [mah-law]…b – d.

LI - - E [lee-breh]…….free, not being used

CERRADO [theh-rad-aw]…closed.

AB - - - T O [ah-bee-her-taw] open.

ENCANTADO [ehn-kahn-tah-daw]…..pleased.

OC – P – DO [aw-koo-pah-daw]……… engaged

PROBIHIDO……………………..(You can guess!)

Now I have to tell you that I HAVE BEEN HIDING SOMETHING FROM YOU! Can you guess what it is?

To make it interesting, choose (a), (b), or (c) from the following guilty secrets:

(i) I have never been to Spain in my life.

ii) I have not told you something important.

(iii) I am really a pop star.

If you have chosen (a) or (c) you only have to ring 017996-3224476-9192855 and listen. The call will cost you an arm and a leg but that serves you right for not choosing (b).

So what is this important information I have been hiding?

Read the following statements:

1. Tengo frío……I am cold 2. Tienes frío…….You are cold

When we mean ' I ' as in 'I have' we use the first part of the verb which ends in 'o' or y'- think of 'estoy, voy, doy, quiero'. This first part of the verb goes with 'yo'.

So " I have" is "Tengo"(yo tengo) . Creo…. (yo creo)I think, I believe. Now guess the following:

Invito – I u- - - - - - - - -   (Yeah, really tough, this one!)

Hablo - I s - - - k.

Espero…….. I h - - - e, I w - - h

Comprendo - I   u - d - - s t a - -

Conecto…………I c - - - - -t (Yeah, sorry again. Another tough one!

To help you still more I list below the full form of the verb before you change it – just fill in the blanks to get their meanings.

SPANISH	ENGLISH
CAMBIAR	C – a – g –
HABLAR	S – e – k
COMPRENDER	U – d – r - - a - d
INVITAR	I know, another toughie!
ESPERAR	Use your dictionary.

Now look back at the sentence number 2 on page 33:

"Tienes frío". 'Tienes' is the second part of the verb, meaning 'you' and goes with ' tú' When do we use it? When speaking to close friends or children (and PETS!!!).

You may now be wondering what we use to address someone who is not a friend - an official, a shop assistant or someone we have not met before......WAIT FOR A LATER CHAPTER !!

*   *   *   *   *   *   *   *   *   *

So just to make it clear, read this conversation:

(Yo) hablo español, pero (yo) no hablo francés.

¿(Tú) hablas francés?

There are 2 main points here (you'll find the

translation if you need it on the last page of this book).

POINT 1. I have put 'yo' and 'tú' in brackets.

Because they are almost always left out in ordinary, everyday speech.

If I say they are not needed, can you think why?

POINT 2. In written Spanish question marks and exclamation marks are written upside down at the beginning of a sentence, as well as in their usual positions at the end of the sentence.

WHY? THINK ABOUT IT. Answer at bottom of this page.

(To let the reader know that a question or exclamation follows.

To make it crystal clear, "Hablo inglés" as it stands can mean:

   (i) I speak English. (ii) Do I speak English. (iii) I (certainly do)speak English.

We can only make the situation clearer by putting in the correct punctuation. Can you write the meanings in (i), (ii) and (iii) below?

  (i)Hablo inglés

  (ii) ¿Hablo inglés?

  (iii)¡Hablo inglés!

Read this conversation:

"Vivo en Madrid. Vives en Madrid. No, vivo en Granada."

Not absolutely clear, is it? It is better with the Spanish punctuation.

  "Vivo en Madrid."

"¿Vives en Madrid?"

"¡No! Vivo en Granada."

The translation is on the last page of this book.

YOU WON'T NEED IT!

CHAPTER SIX

Your 5 words:

Hola [Aw – lah] Go on, guess.

Hasta luego [ah-stah loo-eh gaw]……See you later

¿Cómo estás? [kaw-maw eh-stahs]…..How are you? (Friendly)

We left out ' tú' in the last phrase because we didn't need it. But what about the Spanish words for – he, she, we, they, etc.

You will have to learn these, but REMEMBER - if you really want to learn - YOU WILL.

TEST TIME.

Translate this conversation into Spanish.

"Hello, John. How are you?

"I'm all right (bien), Peter. How are you?"

"I'm all right. Where (Donde) are you going?"

"I'm going shopping."

Now translate this one into English

"Hola, Miguel. ¿ Cómo estás? "

"Muy bien, gracias. ¿Y tú?"

"Estoy bien. ¿Quieres una cerveza?"

"Sí, gracias."

There are NO translations of these conversations, so you'll just have to rely on yourself.

AND I KNOW YOU CAN!!

YOU WILL GET THEM ALL RIGHT.

CHAPTER SEVEN

Many phrase books make the mistake of trying to cover so many situations that they end up by covering none. If you anticipate a situation, you can usually find words you may need in a dictionary or good phrase book, but if, for example, you are robbed in the street or supermarket and then report to the Guardia Civil you will probably find that your phrase book is worse than useless. How would you as an English couple who had been robbed, explain what had happened?

"We were walking along when this young man approached us and asked for a light for his cigarette and while I was looking for my lighter, he stole my wife's handbag."

When this book is issued in a second edition, I will translate that little complaint for you. It could be useful –but I hope not. Most Guardia Civil officers would look at you blankly. I have always found them to be rather stony-faced individuals, and not very sympathetic to foreigners' tales of woe - after all, they hear so many. I have also yet to meet one who speaks English.

In this book I try to give you the essentials of what you NEED. But how do I know? Living in Spain as I do, and having lived and worked in both Madrid and Seville, I have often been asked either to translate or to interpret and the main areas where I have been asked to help seem to be the following:-

1. Basic Asking For.

2. Basic Telling.

3. Giving Information – Understanding.

4. **Dealing with Situations.**

(a) Medical			(e) Accommodation

(b) Shopping & Meals		(f) Banking

(c) Driving			(g) Post Office

(d) Police			(h) Telephone

(i) Robbery

The remainder of this book will deal with these basic situations, so let's start with the ' asking for' situation. You already know how to start – use "quiero" and so, for example:

"Quiero pan/ vino/ un café con leche/ una cerveza

Here are some more examples so see if you can translate them (NO PROBLEM!!) and then learn them……..Back to PAGE 6?

1. Quiero dos cafes y un té

2. Quiero un kilo de patatas

3. ¿ Tiene Vd. un plan (callejero) de Malaga? (street map)

An interesting sentence. Notice the 'Vd.' - the short form of 'usted', the polite form of 'you' (pronunciation(oo-stehd').

4. Déme (please give me/ can I have) un vaso de agua. (This may sound abrupt, but it isn't).

5. ¿ Tienes un boli?   ('boli' – ball-point, 'biro')

Now that you know how to ask for something, it's CRUNCH TIME!!

Learn the following expressions and words,

Quiero, déme, tiene Vd, patata, vaso, plano , and now learn these too:

¿ Cuánto es?

¿Cuánto cuesta?

¿Cuál es el precio?…….All meaning more or less the same, so

GUESS THEIR MEANINGS!

Test.

Translate these into English – then learn and practise the sentences AND put in the correct accent marks.

¿ Cuanto cuesta esta blusa?

If 'esta' means 'this'. What does 'está' mean? 'He/ she/ it IS' Which would you choose?

¿ Cual es el precio de este televisor? (Now note 'esta' and 'este' both mean 'this' but which is masculine and which feminine?)

Déme una taza de té y dos cafés.

IMPORTANT…..Coffee in Spanish bars is almost always served in a glass and sometimes too hot to manage.. You can ask for a cup. HOW?

It is not unusual to hear in a bar, "¡Oiga! Déme una cerveza…"

In England we would call for attention by using one of the
following:

"Excuse me! Shop! Hello!" Or just, "Oi!"

I find that in Spain, a quiet " Oiga" with the stress on the 'a' is sufficient to get attention.

More words for shopping & eating:

Garlic – ajo [ah-haw].   **Ham – jamón [hah-mawn]**

Juice – zumo [thoo-maw]

Ice-cream – helado [eh-lah-daw]

Apple – manzana [mah- thahn-ah].

Peach – melocotón [mehl-aw-kaw-tawn].

Pear – pera [peh-rah].

Pineapple – piña [peen-yah]

Rice - arroz [ahrr-awth].

Cream – nata [nah-tah]

Egg – huevo [weh-vaw]   **Salt – sal [sahl]**

Lamb – cordero [kawr-deh-raw]

Pork – cerdo [thehr-daw]

Meals & eating:

Eat – comer [kaw – mehr]   **Meal – comida [kaw-mee-dah]**

Dessert – postre [paw – streh]

Time & Distance:

Morning, tomorrow: mañana

Evening, tarde [tahr-deh].

Near – cerca [thehr- kah-]

Far – lejos [leh – hos]

Driving: conducir – [kawn –doo-theer]

Driving licence, permiso de conducir [pehr-mee-saw deh -………..]

Engine, motor [maw –tawr]

Switch on engine: arrancar [ahr –kahn-kar]

poner en marcha [paw-nehr ehn marh-chah]

Switch off engine: parar [pah –rahr]

Wheel: rueda [roo–eh-dah]

Jack: gato [gah –taw] (Yes it's the same word for 'cat' the feline.

Tyre: pneumatico [neh – oo – mah - tee- kaw]

CHAPTER EIGHT

BASIC TELLING:

This chapter will deal with basic ' telling' situations, where you give information about yourself or your circumstances in the following situations.

1. At the police station.   2. At the medical centre.

3. at the hospital.

To my mind, these are the basic telling situations.

Now I'm asking you to start thinking in Spanish. Start by looking around you and saying the Spanish words for what you see and progress from words to phrases, e., taza – veo una taza – veo una taza grande en la mesa.

Let's go back to the beginning of this chapter and think of the information we would usually give in those situations. It is usually...

Name –apellido (ah-pehl-yee-daw)

So the conversation may go,

Official: " ¿Cómo se llama Vd?" [kaw-maw seh lyamah oostethd]
What's your name? or ¿Su apellido?
Answer: Me llamo.....[meh lyam-aw]
Official: ¿Cuál es su dirección?....What is your address

For medical care, you may choose to rely on the private sector or on the state health service. I use the latter and am well satisfied not only by its high standards, but also for the opportunities it gives me to listen to people, to speak to them and to involve myself in everyday Spanish life. To use the state service you have to register with your local health centre [centro de salud]. Most have interpreters, but as they are almost always volunteers, it is a good idea to take someone with you who speaks Spanish. Failing that, try saying,

"Habla más despacio…" and just hope for the best!

THAT IS WHY IT IS SO VERY IMPORTANT TO HAVE SOME SPANISH FOR THE CRISIS TIMES!!

At the centro de salud after you have provided your basic details and filled in a form to register[rellenar un impreso] in order to join the centre –(' darse de alta'), you should ask for a 'cita' [thee-tah] to see a octor. Your 'cita' (appointment) is usually a small piece of paper bearing a time for you to see the doctor and a number.

You guard it with your life, not only for its importance, but because it also gives you an 'in' to the 'circle of the sick'

"¿Qué número tiene Vd?" If someone does not ask you this, you will almost certainly hear it. I was propositioned once in such a circle!

When you see the doctor, you may be lucky and find one who speaks English, although many read and understand it, but the modern Spaniard's basic (and perfectly understandable attitude) was expressed by a young lady doctor I spoke to a few months ago. I had asked her,

"¿Habla Vd. inglés?" and her answer was concise,

"¿Por qué? Vivo aquí en España."

(Come on, translate. I know you can!)

Now look up the following:

Doctor…………….. Nurse………………………

The head…………..

El brazo............[brah-thaw]

El estómago [ehs-taw-mah-gaw]……………..

Why have I included the 'el/la' with the Spanish words? The reason is that in Spanish we say "The foot hurts me." NOT 'my foot hurts.' The formula is – "Me duele la cabeza." – [my head hurts].

'doler' comes from the verb 'doler' (think of the word 'doleful')

Now translate:

I have a pain in my back.

Me…d…………la…e……………………………

My arm hurts………………………………………………………….

.

I have a pain in my leg…M…d…l……????????…………………………

…….

Where is the medical centre?

………………………………………………….

Look up the following:

Hand, foot, ankle, leg, wrist.

Now answer these questions:

¿Cómo se llama Vd?

¿Cúal es su dirección?

Now give your address in Spain and maybe explain that you are on holiday (estoy de vacaciones , ehs-toy deh vah-kah-thee-aw-nehs)

I promised earlier to let you know when to use 'usted'. The answer is quite simple – use it with anyone to whom you have just been introduced, to someone in authority, a member of a profession (medical or otherwise).

If you do have to be admitted to hospital, DO NOT WORRY.

Spanish hospitals compare very well to those in the U.K. and are of a uniformly very high standard and any reports I have had from British friends are completely positive.

CHAPTER NINE

UNDERSTANDING:

By this I mean two things (a) understanding what is said to you and (b) understanding written notices.

Let's take the second one and I will give you a list of words (more than the usual 5, I'm afraid). You will just have to learn them BUT don't make hard work of it. Learn 2/3 a day.

PICTURE YOURSELF SPEAKING FLUENT SPANISH>

WORD	MEANING	EXAMPLE
1.CUIDADO	CAUTION	CUIDADO
OBRAS	Work in Progress	

2. PELIGRO   DANGER

CURVA PELIGROSA   (Think about it!)

3. ATENCIÓN AL PERRO   Beware of   ATENCIÓN

4. CERRADO   CLOSED

5. ABIERTO   OPEN

6. AVERIADO   OUT OF ORDER

7. ASCENSOR   LIFT

8. TIRAR   PULL   Almost always on doors

9. EMPUJAR   PUSH   Also on doors

10. PARADA   BUS STOP

11. SERVICIOS   TOILETS/WASH ROOM   See note ** below

12. DAMAS/SEÑORAS   LADIES

13. CABALLEROS   Gentlemen

14. SE VENDE   For Sale

15. SE ALQUILA   To rent

   (ahl-kee-lah)

16. APARCAMIENTO   Parking

As well as learning these words, you should know how they are pronounced. All the pronunciation guides are listed below, labeled a – p, so all you have to do is match the pronunciation with its corresponding word in the list above numbered 1 – 16. If, for

example, you think that (a) in the list below goes with 12, then write that number beside (a).

   (a) ah-sen-thawr   (b) seh vehn-deh

   (c) ah-pahr-kah-mee-en-taw

(d) ah-tehn-thee-awn   ahl pehr-rawh

(e) theh-rah-daw   (f) tee-rahr

(g) sehr-vee-thee-aws   (h) pah- radth-ah

(i) dah-mahs/ sehn-yaw-rahs

(j) ehm-poo-hahr

(k) kwee-dah-daw

(l) peh-lee-graw

(m) kah-bahl-yehr-aws

(n) seh-ahl-kee-lahr

(o) ah-bee-ehr-taw

(p) ah-vehr-ee-ah-daw

Just before we finish this bit, there are two points to mention.

1. The Spanish 'd' sound is much softer than in English so when speaking Spanish I always pronounce 'nada' as [nah-thah] as in 'no pasa nada'. Try practising it. Getting that sound right will endear you to Spanish friends for nothing sounds more awful than to hear 'nada' pronounced as ' naDa'. ('D'for 'dummy')

2. The Spanish 'j' is not easy (unless you are Scots like me, so in the pronunciation guide I have shown it as 'h' , but sounded with a rasp in the throat. Try saying 'loch' as the Scots say it and remember it is NOT 'lock'!!!

   ** You will also see the sign 'Aseos' but if you are in a bar/restaurant and want the toilet, just say, "Hay servicios? /Donde estan los servicios?

CHAPTER TEN

Chapter 9 was rather long and had a lot of things for you to remember, but that will make things easier for you now. What I suggest you do while you are getting to grips with (getting your head round) all I've told you) is to have some fun. Play word games with your partner/ friend along the lines of I-Spy. I know it sounds flaky, naff or childish, but if it helps, what does it matter? Here are 6 words to learn (and you can use them in I-Spy!!)

Marido, esposa, novio, novia, amigo, amiga)

You find the meanings!

Another game is to say a Spanish word to your partner. They have to write down its English equivalent – a test of your pronunciation. When you've said about 10, check them and then swap over   and if you have said 'amigo' [ah-mee-gaw] and your mate has written 'husband' then you both have a problem.

I DID PROMISE TO EXPLAIN A LITTLE MORE ABOUT 'BEEB' – REMEMBER?

I now want to remind you about the last 'B' standing for 'BODY' and to say that if you involve

as much of your body while you are learning, ii will be easier for you and that what you learn will be more easily recalled.

I also promised that you WOULD learn Spanish. How did I know? Well, unless you have jumped off a cliff or have given up learning Spanish altogether, then that proves that you have the will to learn….and IF YOU WANT TO……YOU WILL!!

Let's deal with another situation, and it's a very basic one – understanding what is said to you. We all speak our own language quickly and it can be daunting to have someone address you and not to understand one single word. So what can you do? First of all, ask them to speak more slowly (you will find the phrase you need in the section dealing with medical centre) or you can pretend to be deaf and say, "¿Cómo?" This is usually used to ask someone to repeat what he/she has said. That should work, but if it doesn't, just say,

"No comprendo." You must then hope that you'll get a result.

SHOPPING: Make this easier for yourself by listing in Spanish all that you wish to buy. Use your dictionary (if you have to) and have the phrases ready that I gave you earlier. If you do your shopping this way it may be difficult at first – it's so easy just to scribble, 'bread, marge, spuds, veg, bleach.'

But doing that will make your learning process very much longer AND more difficult.

CHAPTER ELEVEN

Driving, the police, and some other things:

This could be a long chapter, but I'll keep it short.

(1) When driving remember to keep STRICTLY to speed limits. I drove a RHD vehicle earlier his year and they attract the Guardia Civil like wasps to a honey-pot. I was closely followed by a GC 4x4 for 10 km. They usually come down like a ton of bricks on speeding foreigners.

(2) DO I NEED TO SAY remember to drive on the right? It's no problem except when you have just entered a side road from a main one, or vice-versa.

There are 2 types of police in Spain, the ordinary local police who function more or less like our own 'bobbies' (El Cuerpo Nacional de Policia) – dark-blue uniforms, they deal with traffic, small traffic 'foul-ups' and petty crime, whereas the main function of the Guardia Civil (light olive green uniform) is to secure Spain's borders on land and at sea. They are rather like the French 'gendarmerie', a semi-military police force that had a reputation of being pretty tough 'hombres'. They deal with robbery and will be very helpful – if you speak Spanish!!

3. OTHER THINGS:

I did not want this book to be too long nor too large so we're coming to the end of our journey together – an exploration of YOUR POWER to LEARN. I have to cover only 4 more topics.

Accommodation. If you arranged your holiday through a travel company then this will have been taken care of, but for those who wish to arrange their own accommodation, you have 3 choices:

paradors – government sponsored hotels and usually very good value for money. Then there are the multitude of hotels and you have to decide what star rating to go for, last but not least are the 'hostales' which I suppose we would call 'boarding houses'. They are usually cheap, very clean and can provide meals at reasonable cost.

One last suggestion: if on your travels you spot a 'mesón', don't pass it. They usually offer good Spanish food at very reasonable cost. My husband and I found an excellent one in Almonte, a small family restaurant (they used to be called 'casa de comidas') and the father who cooked, invited us into the kitchen to choose what we wanted to eat. Unforgettable!)

BANKING:

I seldom have to queue at my bank. They open at 8-30 a.m. and close at 2 and branches in large towns usually have someone who speaks English but here are some words that should come in useful:

Ingresar…x……euros(?) en una cuenta

[een-greh-sahr..eh-oo-raws ehn oonah kwehn-tah] – To deposit….€x? into an account.

Importe [eem-pawr-teh] – amount, cost, value (you see this on receipts from stores and supermarkets).

Factura – [fahk-too-rah] bill

Example: Debo pagar la factura de telefónica –I should pay my telephone bill.
On the phone: When you pick up the receiver to answer a call, say, "Diga/ digame." (Please speak – slightly less illogical than 'Hello'!)

If you are making a call, you wait until the receiver is picked up at the other end and then you say,

"Oiga" which I have explained before.

THE LAST PAGE –WELL ALMOST!

Translations:

p.35. I speak Spanish but I don't speak French.

Do you speak French?

p.23. I live in Madrid. Do you live in Madrid?

No. I live in Granada.

As promised – words referring to persons:

Yo [yaw]   You (informal) tú   He/it….él/ lo

She/it…..Ella/la   You (formal) usted [Vd]

We…….nosotros   You……(informal)….vosotros

They (masculine)….ellos[ehl-yaws]

They (feminine)…..GUESS THIS ONE………….

You (formal) Ustedes (Vds)

Example: "Quiero decir a Vds. abogados…"

"I want to tell you lawyers…"

That word 'abogado' is similar to the English word 'advocate'. Yes?

Just a few useful words to finish:

All – todo el mundo (everybody) Also – tambien

Always – siempre   Cheap – barato

Chemist – farmacia

Now I hear a voice asking, "Where's the phrase book?"
You may have gathered that I'm not a fan of phrase books and I think the best 'phrase list' is the one inside your head. A dictionary is handy but a phrase book may prove not to be as useful as you thought.

Two final things to set you on your way:

1. The word 'hay' [pronounced as 'I' in 'I am'] is incredibly useful, so:

"Are there any toilets here?" –

Hay servicios aquí? [I sehr-vee-thee-aws   ah-kee]

(There is a missing punctuation mark in that sentence. Can you find it?)

You will find the little word 'se' very handy. Read through the following examples then make up some of your own (the formula is always the same.)

'se puede' + full form of the verb

or 'se' + 3rd bit of the full verb – the bit that goes with 'usted, él, ella.'

Here are the examples:

¿Se habla inglés?…[seh ah-blah een-glehs] Do you/ Does anyone speak English?

¿Se puede entrar…[seh poo-ehd-eh ehn-trahr]…Can I / we come in?

¿Se puede pagar con tarjeta?[…..pah-gahr kawn tahr-heta]. Can I pay with my card?

¿Se espera aquí? [...ehs-peh-rah ah- kee]...May I/he/ she, etc wait here?

¿Se vende (este apartamento)?[...vehn-deh eh-steh] Easy to guess...

¿Se alquila esta casa?[...ahl-kee-lah...]
…………………………..

I could give you many, many more but as YOU know best what is right for YOU then I will finish here and say,

¡S U E R T E !

THE   END

www.ingramcontent.com/pod-product-compliance
Ingram Content Group UK Ltd.
Pitfield, Milton Keynes, MK11 3LW, UK
UKHW021322180426
11947UKWH00015B/1381